RETURN

Remarks on the Condition of Slaves in Jamaica

William Sells

Remarks on the Condition of the Slaves in the Island of Jamaica

Irish University Press

Shannon Ireland

First edition: London 1823

This IUP reprint is a photolithographic
facsimile of the first edition and is
unabridged, retaining the original imprints.

© 1972 *Irish University Press Shannon Ireland*

All forms of micropublishing
© *Irish University Microforms Shannon Ireland*

ISBN 0 7165 0120 1

T. M. MacGlinchey Publisher
Irish University Press Shannon Ireland

Printed in the Republic of Ireland by
Robert Hogg Printer to Irish University Press

REMARKS

ON THE

CONDITION OF THE SLAVES

IN THE

Island of Jamaica.

BY

WILLIAM SELLS,

MEMBER OF THE ROYAL COLLEGE OF SURGEONS, LONDON; AND
MANY YEARS PRACTITIONER IN THE PARISH OF CLARENDON,
IN THE ISLAND OF JAMAICA.

LONDON:

PRINTED FOR J. M. RICHARDSON, CORNHILL, AND
RIDGWAYS, PICCADILLY.

1823.

Price 1s. 6d.

HUGHES, Printer,
Maiden Lane, Covent Garden.

CONTENTS.

ADVERTISEMENT.

———

THE writer of the following Remarks having lately arrived from Jamaica, and having his attention drawn to the discussion that has been for some time pending on the subject of the condition of the negroes in our sugar colonies, observed with great surprise the degree of error in the opinions prevalent on the subject. No one seemed to be apprised of the improvements that had, of late years, taken place in the condition of the negroes; nor of the important fact, that they enjoy a portion of comfort, which, as far as physical wants are concerned, is decidedly superior to that of a great portion of the labouring classes in this country. The existing impressions appear, in a great measure, founded on

B

a few publications, extensively circulated; in particular, Mr. Wilberforce's Appeal; Mr. Macauley's Treatise on Negro Slavery; and the Notes added to the printed copy of the Debate in the House of Commons, on the 15th May last. These publications he will now pass briefly in review, and expose a few of the points in which exaggeration has been carried to a striking length.

REMARKS,

&c. &c.

----◆----

THAT the Author of the following pages has had opportunities of obtaining knowledge upon those points respecting which he is about to offer his testimony, may be admitted, when he informs the Public that he has been engaged from the middle of the year 1803, until May 1823, in the discharge of his professional duties in the interior of Jamaica, and has been, during the greater part of that period, in very extensive practice. Having made nearly a final settlement of his affairs in the West Indies, and having no further interest there, directly or indirectly, personally or otherwise, he comes forward without solicitation, and from no motive whatever, but to serve the *cause of genuine universal truth and justice.*

8

It is easy to indulge in declamation against slavery, as who can be found to approve of it in the abstract? Mr. Wilberforce, when he says, that " few of our countrymen are at all apprised " of the actual condition of the bulk of the " negro population," and when, by the conceal- ment of some facts, and the gross exaggeration of others, he endeavours to rouse their passions upon the subject, is well aware how few of them are acquainted with the origin and history of the slave trade in the West Indies; and how great a portion of the guilt, if guilt it must be called, of establishing the colonies by the labour of slaves, attaches to the government and people of this country, as may be clearly shewn by numerous Orders in Council and Acts of Parlia- ment.* To draw down odium upon the West

* In Mr. Barham's pamphlet, entitled, " Considerations on the Abolition of Negro Slavery," is the following striking and very convincing statement of historical facts.

" Great Britain established the slave trade in the reign of Queen Elizabeth, who person- ally took a share in it.

" The colonies did not then exist.

" Great Britain encouraged it in the successive reigns of Charles I., Charles II., and James II., by every means that could be devised. But it was William III. who outdid them

" The colonies, all this time, took no share in it themselves, merely purchasing what the British merchants brought them, and doing therein what the British Government in-

Indians, Mr. Wilberforce dwells particularly upon the state of the negroes at a period when

all. With Lord Somers for his minister, he declared the slave trade to be ' highly beneficial to the nation.' By the Assiento Treaty, in 1713, with which the colonies had nothing to do, Great Britain binds herself to supply 144,000 slaves, at the rate of £4,800 per annum, to the Spanish colonies.

vited them to do, by every means in their power.

" So much as to those who created and fostered the trade; and now let us see who it was that first marked it with disapprobation, and sought to confine it within narrower bounds.

" The colonies began in 1760. South Carolina (then a British colony) passed an act to prohibit further importation; but

" Great Britain rejected this act with indignation, and declared that the slave trade was beneficial and necessary to the mother country. The governor who passed it was reprimanded, and a circular was sent to all other governors, warning them against a similar offence.

" The colonies, however, in 1765, repeated the offence, and a bill was twice read in the Assembly of Jamaica, for the same purpose of limiting the importation of slaves; when

" Great Britain stopped it, through the governor of that island, who sent for the Assembly, and told them that, consistently with his instructions, he could not give his assent, upon which the bill was dropped.

even the inhabitants of this now happy land were without practical liberty, and before we were in possession of our Bill of Rights.

Mr. Wilberforce, in his Appeal, and Mr. Buxton, in his Speech, would impress the Public with a belief that little or nothing has been done towards mitigating the condition of the slave; although they should and do well know, that much has been accomplished during the last fifteen years, and that the work of amelioration has not only commenced, but has made such a progress as might bid effectual defiance to any attempts which could be made to arrest its

" The colonies, in 1774, tried once more, and the Assembly of Jamaica actually passed two bills to restrict the trade; but

"The colonies, by the agent of Jamaica, remonstrated against that report, and pleaded against it on all the grounds of justice and humanity; but

" Great Britain again resisted the restriction. Bristol and Liverpool petitioned against it. The matter was referred to the Board of Trade, and that Board reported against it.

" Great Britain, by the mouth of the Earl of Dartmouth, then President of the Board, answered by the following declaration: — ' We ' cannot allow the colonists ' to check or discourage, i.. ' any degree, a traffic so'bene- ' ficial to the nation.' And this was in 1774!"—*Vide p.* 27—29.

course, unless diverted by rash and ill informed interference.

It is proposed to describe, first, the condition of slaves, as regards the means they now possess of supplying their physical wants; and to begin with the article of Food. For some years after the Author went to Jamaica, owing to continued new importations of negroes, to a sudden and greatly extended demand for provisions, and to the occasional failure of periodical rains, many suffered from an inadequate supply; but of late, the negro character has much improved; they are more industrious; and having twenty-six days in the year, exclusive of Sundays and holidays, for cultivating their grounds and gardens, want is almost entirely unknown to them. Of this we had a strong proof, in the very severe and long-continued drought of 1821.

Visitors in Jamaica, who have witnessed the vast quantities of provisions, vegetables, and fruits, brought to Kingston market, by the slaves from the surrounding country, have been truly astonished at the proofs thus afforded of a surplus produce beyond the negro consumption. The money these articles produce, is laid out in fine clothing, trinkets, &c. The same remark applies to the markets in other towns, and in the interior; few negroes are without poultry, and great numbers have pigs. The Author's family (like many other families in the island) was supplied with pork, poultry, eggs, corn, pulse, and other articles, by the negro slaves in the neighbourhood. This is a practical contradiction to the abstract theory respecting the " minimum of food," which Mr. Wilberforce would have his readers believe is the lot of the field negro or labourer. In the towns, and in many families in the country, the slaves have a weekly allowance of money, to feed themselves; and which has, within the last twenty years, been encreased from three or four bits, (about 1s. 9d. sterling,) to half a dollar, (about 2s. 3d. sterling,) for each person, old and young; 3s. 6d. sterling, in Kingston, is very general; and a dollar, or 4s. 6d. sterling, to head servants. Provisions are much cheaper now than formerly; clothing, especially printed cottons, also cheaper than when their allowance was little more than the half of what it is now; consequently, they have it in their power to make considerable savings, which they dispose of in buying articles for dress, of a finer description than those which they receive from their masters, and subscribe towards the building of places of worship, and the maintenance of the ministers who officiate in them.

As to their Clothing, the Author considers

that he cannot do better than give the following
extract from the Report of the Jamaica House
of Assembly, of 1815,* on this subject, assuring
his readers that it is *sober* truth. " The clothing
" given is abundant for the wants of the climate.
" It is to be understood that the clothes distri-
" buted by the master are of a plain, substantial
" kind, such as are worn when at labour; but
" every negro, with the exception of a few idle
" and disorderly persons, from which that class of
" mankind is not exempt, has better clothes,
" which are worn on holidays and festivals; and
" the appearance of the population of all old
" settled estates, dressed in their best apparel,
" would, on such an occasion, excite the asto-
" nishment of a zealous abolitionist, who might
" fancy himself transported into the court of an
" African prince, when he found dancing, revel-
" ling, humour, and mimicry, in place of stripes,
" groans, and misery, which his heated imagina-
" tion had anticipated. Every candid European
" acknowledges how much, and how agreeably
" he is disappointed, by the first appearance of
" the negro population, not merely in hours of
" festivity, but at plantation labour, and when

* A reference to this Report would satisfy the reader that
the evidence there detailed was the most unexceptionable
which could be obtained; consisting, in great part, of the
testimony of the most disinterested and respectable persons
in the island.

" conducting their own affairs in the public
" markets." With respect to Houses and Fuel,
little need be said on those topics; the former
are comfortable, the latter is abundant.

" There is no plantation where a Hospital is
" not provided, and generally on an extensive
" scale, and under good regulations, in respect to
" cleanliness and ventilation. A regularly bred
" practitioner attends; the master supplying not
" only medicines, but the comforts required for
" persons in such a situation. Wine, rice, flour,
" sugar, and animal food, are provided; and it is
" an invariable rule, if a well-disposed negro pre-
" sent himself at the hospital, never to repulse
" him, although both the doctor and the overseer
" be satisfied that he is not labouring under any
" real sickness, but wishes a day's rest and
" relaxation."*

Since the Author first began practice in
Jamaica, hospitals are much better constructed,
and are supplied with more efficient nurses.
The regular visits of the medical attendant have
been encreased from once or twice weekly, to
one every or every other day, in the ordinary
routine of business, besides answering promptly
all calls on particular emergencies. Hospital

* Island Report.

journals (formerly kept in a slovenly manner)
have been more carefully conducted,* and
more attention paid to carrying the doctor's
prescriptions and directions into effect, than
heretofore.

As regards the treatment of Pregnant Women, he will add, from the before-mentioned
Report, an extract from the evidence he gave
before the Committee of the House of Assembly,
Nov. 17, 1815, in reply to the following question:—" What is the mode of treatment which
" you consider best, and have recommended to
" be observed on the estates under your care, in
" respect of women who are pregnant, and
" during the period when they are suckling
" children? Have you found a general disposi-
" tion to attend to such recommendation on the
" part of the proprietors and managers of
" estates? and have such or similar plans been
" commonly followed of late years? and do you
" or do you not believe that they will soon be
" very generally or universally followed?—
" A. Examinant saith, he has lately directed
" his attention a great deal to the subject of
" this question, and has thought that the adop-
" tion of the plan he is about to describe may
" be productive of great good; viz. the having

* See Table I. at the end of this Pamphlet.

" proper lying-in houses, with apartments ac-
" cording to the number of breeding women on
" the estate, and a room to be employed as a
" nursery; the women to lye-in *there*, (instead
" of going to their own houses,) *where* they
" would be more likely to receive better atten-
" tion than in their own houses, from the
" manager and the medical practitioner. He
" would also recommend the children being
" weaned after from nine to twelve months'
" suckling, (provided there be nothing in the
" state of the child's health to forbid it,) and
" kept together in the nursery. Further, that
" examinant has advised lists being kept of the
" breeding women in columns, thus*--the wo-
" man's name, her age, when she reports herself
" pregnant, how far gone with child, whether
" she is liable to abortion, and a memorandum
" of its causes; what number of children she
" has living; when delivered, the sex of the
" child, the state of the mother and infant at the
" end of the month, with occasional remarks.
" This plan has but lately occurred to exami-
" nant, and he is glad to say it is now in pro-
" gress on Kellitt's Estate, the property of
" Mr. Shand, where it promises to be productive
" of the desired effects. The medical attendant
" giving his attention to such an arrangement,

* See Table II.

" by frequently seeing the women during their
" pregnancy, has opportunities of giving the
" managers instructions for their government
" during that period. He purposes to recom-
" mend a similar establishment upon other pro-
" perties; and has no doubt that his recom-
" mendation will be generally adopted. With
" respect to the labour of women during preg-
" nancy, unless where liability to abortion, or
" constitutional weakness, forbids it, examinant
" recommends no alteration in their usual labour,
" until four or five months advanced; a lighter
" employment is then advised, and continued
" until the period of lying-in. The advantages
" of the above plan he considers far greater
" than any that can accrue from allowing what
" is called further indulgence. Examinant has
" generally met with great readiness from pro-
" prietors and managers of estates, to adopt any
" advice he has given for the treatment of
" women so circumstanced. He sees no reason
" to alter the usual practice of the lying-in
" woman going to her usual work, after a month
" or six weeks from the time of delivery, pro-
" vided nothing peculiar in the state of her
" health forbids it."

In conformity with the foregoing evidence,
he soon afterwards published his " Practical
" Remarks for the management of Pregnant

" Women, &c." with tables corresponding with
the form before described, and introduced the
following paragraph. " So strongly is the writer
" impressed with the utility of lying-in houses,
" that he believes on their establishment taking
" place, and *properly instructed midwives being*
" *provided, (a matter deserving most serious atten-*
" *tion, and without which all else can be of no*
" *avail,)* tetanus, or lock-jaw, would become
" almost as rare among negro as among white
" infants. The mischievous results of this
" destructive malady would be made apparent,
" were it a practice of managers of estates, in
" keeping their increase and decrease lists, to
" enter all births, and not, as is too common a
" practice, to omit taking any notice of such as
" die within the ninth day. It would also be
" well to state the age of every negro who dies,
" as nearly as possible, in such lists." According
with these suggestions, of late years several
excellent lying-in houses have been constructed
in the Parish of Clarendon, where the writer
resided, and many women educated as midwives
at considerable expence; there is now a greater
proportion of intelligent creole mothers, and
children are better taken care of than formerly.

While on this subject, it will not perhaps be
misplaced, to introduce part of a paper which
the Author had printed in the Royal Gazette of

February, 1819:—" The following statements
" shew what diseases prevailed, and the amount
" of mortality in a district of the Parish of Cla-
" rendon, during the year 1818. Their utility
" may not at first view appear considerable, and
" yet it seems not improbable that were medical
" gentlemen to direct their attention to the pro-
" curing and arranging materials for similar
" tables, it would, by presenting to our view in
" the aggregate, the deaths occasioned by cer-
" tain complaints, draw the observation, and
" exercise the ingenuity of the physician, more
" particularly, to attain improvement in the
" modes of treating many ailments, and thereby
" render essential service to the cause of
" humanity.

" Negro Population of the district referred to, on 1st January, 1818 . 5042

" Ditto, ditto, 1st January, 1819 . 5063

" Births in the year 1818 . . 162

" Deaths,   ditto,   ditto . 141

" Increase, being somewhat less than half
 per cent. . . . 21

" Died within the month . . 8
" Do. within the year . . 14
" Between 1 & 5 years . . 16
　　　　5 & 10 ditto . . 11
　　　　10 & 20 ditto . . 12
　　　　20 & 30 ditto . . 20
　　　　30 & 40 ditto . . 14
　　　　40 & 50 ditto . . 9
　　　　50 & 60 ditto . . 25
　　　　60 & 70 ditto . . 7
　　　　70 & 80 ditto . . 3
　　　　80 & 90 ditto . . 2
　　　　　　　　　　　　　──
　　　　　　　　　　　　141
　　　　　　　　　　　　──

" Diseases, &c.

" Aged and invalided . . . 29
" Apoplexy and suddenly . . 5
" Asthma 1
" Cachexies (i. e. bad habit of body) . 13
" Childbed 3
" Consumption . · . . 7
" Convulsions 4
" Dirt eating 2
" Dropsy 6
" Dysentery 3
" Epilepsy 2
" Eruptive disease . . . 1
　　　　　　　　　　　　──
　　Carry forward . . 76

Brought forward	.	.	76
" Fever	.	.	.	10
" Hæmorrhage	.	.	.	1
" Influenza	.	.	.	4
" Lues	.	.	.	2
" Marasmus	.	.	.	4
" Peripneumony and Pleurisy	.	.	5
" Scirrhus Pylorus	.	.	.	2
" Teething	.	.	.	1
" Trismus (lock-jaw)	.	.	.	4
" Worms	.	.	.	8
" Yaws	.	.	.	6
" Died within the month	.	.	8
" Killed by lightning	.	.	1
" Drowned	.	.	.	2
" Run over by Waggons	.	.	3
" Overlaid	.	.	.	2
" Suicides	.	.	.	2
				141 "

It was always the opinion of the writer that an increase of population among the negro slaves could be accomplished only after the lapse of some time, and *that* he would now look forward to at an early period. Acute disease is now more attended to in its commencement; and chronic disease, as influenced by carelessness or harshness, much less frequent.

c

Mr. Wilberforce's observation, that the "maximum" of Labour is obtained from negroes, is not correct; that of the Rev. Mr. Bridges is much nearer the truth, when he says, that "Two " of the most effective of them would not turn " over as much ground in your garden in one " day, as your own gardener does, *cæteris paribus*, " in half that time; that, in short, no comparison " of manual labour, which you can contemplate, " holds good between the negro and the day- " labourer in England, who will reap an acre of " wheat between day-light and sun-set."

From the manner in which the driving system is described, and the frequent repetition of the words whip and cart whip, the reader would suppose that the driver need be indeed an *athletic* man, to go through the fatigue which such incessant whipping would occasion. That Mr. Wilberforce's account of the driver's exercise of his authority, in the use of " this dreadful " instrument of punishment, in the shockingly " indecent manner," so feelingly depicted, is exaggerated, and that he has selected particular instances of cruelty, and given them to the world as the general and universal practice, may be credited, when the writer asserts, that during his long residence in Jamaica, he did not meet with half a dozen instances of punishment which would justify such a description. The ordinary use of the whip in the driver's hands is that of cracking it upon the careless and the idle, outside their loose woollen clothing, as they stand up in the field, or elsewhere. Upon many estates, there is no flogging with the cart whip, as it is called; and switching delinquents with a rod is substituted for it.

There is now much less punishment than formerly, both in regard to frequency and quantity. Negroes are become more intelligent beings, and if ill used, go to a magistrate and make known their grievances, which are patiently heard, and should their complaints be well founded, are protected accordingly.

A reader of the Appeal would be tempted to think that a whip, as applied to human beings, is an instrument peculiar to the West Indies; and that we had no whipping in the schools, in the army, in the navy, or in the gaols of Great Britain and Ireland.

When speaking on the subject of labour, it should be remembered, that an extensive and encreasing use of the plough, *drawn by cattle*, in Jamaica, has considerably superseded the digging of cane holes with the hoe.

As far as the writer's experience goes, he

may assert, that when removing negroes, subsequent to a sale, or on being transferred from one property to another, it is quite unusual to separate children from their parents. Families are invariably disposed of together; and it is very rarely indeed that a gang of negroes is removed from one estate to another, without measures being deliberately taken for obtaining their consent. The Author has chanced to see a copy of a letter from an agent in Jámaica to a merchant in London, in which there is the following passage, corroborative of his statement on this subject. " We beg leave to annex a duplicate of " our last letter to you, dated 16th ult., and we " now regret to have to state, that we have been " disappointed in our hopes of obtaining for " Mr. ———'s estates, the gang of negroes we " mentioned. So unanimous and obstinate were " they in their determination not to remove to " —— parish, that we could not prevail upon a " deputation from among them, to go up and " survey the premises; and we were therefore " obliged to relinquish all further idea of their " purchase for these properties."

That the evidence of negroes is not admissible against free persons, is true; it is one of the inevitable results of their condition, and of the relation in which they stand to the general population of the colony; but these causes will gradually cease to operate, when the civilization of the slaves has continued a while longer in its present progressive state, and a competent religious instruction has impressed upon their minds the sacred obligation of an oath.

We will now go somewhat into the subject of the intellectual and moral condition of the negro slave, after first adverting to some passages in the Appeal. Mr. W. says, " It is true, " that low in point of morals as the Africans " may have been in their own country, their " descendants are still lower;" and repeats from Mr. Parke, "that of 130 negroes in a slave ship, " 25 could *most* of them write a *little* Arabic." It is well known that some few of the Mandingoes, and other tribes bordering on the districts inhabited by the Moors, and having intercourse with them, do learn something of their language, and carry pieces of paper or parchment, on which are written Moorish characters, about their persons, and which are supposed to operate as charms, by protecting the wearers against injuries of all sorts; but very few can *read* the language.

Mr. Wilberforce says, " Compare the moral " nature of the Africans, while yet living in " their native land, with the same in our West " Indian colonies, and you will find those in " Africa are *represented* to be industrious, gene-

" rous, eminent for truth, seldom chargeable
" with licentiousness, distinguished for their
" domestic affections, and capable of acts of
" heroic magnanimity." What a captivating
picture this of a people who he assures us, in
one place, "were immersed in all the darkness
" and abominations of paganism." Would it be
too much to ask Mr. Wilberforce, if he believes
on this point, what he would fain induce others
to believe? And have we not, for one account
that gives this favourable character of the inhabitants of Africa, nineteen which give the very
reverse? Are they not rather eminent for indo-
lence, theft, lying, and gross voluptuousness?
And is there no longer such tyranny and cruelty
practised there as is related in Dalzell's Account
of his Embassy to Abomey, the capital of
Dahomey; of the king having ordered a survey
of the court-yard, and other parts contiguous to
the palace, which were covered with human
skulls, and then *out of repair*, in order to ascer-
tain the number of heads which were required
to replace those damaged or missing, and which
was carried into execution accordingly, at the
expence of some 150 lives?

When Mr. Wilberforce was making extracts
from Mr. Long's book, he was aware that his
readers in general knew no distinction between
Negroes and Hottentots; and it is certainly true,
that more than one of the most eminent physio-

logists of the present day believe and teach, that negroes are an inferior grade of the human race; and they draw this conclusion from considering their general history, in connection with the peculiarities of their anatomical structure;* and yet it seems to be expected that the negro should attain the eminence of moral dignity by rapid steps. How much of this moral dignity of man do we find among the greater part of the population of Ireland, Spain, Italy, and Russia?—countries, most of which are old in the march of mind and civilization. In truth, how superior is the character of barbarous Africans, as drawn by Mr. Wilberforce, to that of the most catholic and polished people of Italy! That the utmost degree of moral licentiousness is compatible with much ceremonious (for it cannot be called practical) religion, we have abundant evidence in the capital of the Christian world; and that it may be co-existent with the highest degree of political freedom, we have ample proof in the capital of the Commercial world.

It may appear a bold attempt, but a few words shall be devoted to something like a comparative estimate of the morality of these lowly degraded beings in the West Indies, and

* See White on the Gradations of Man; and the article *Man* in Rees's Cyclopædia.

the highly civilized, religiously and morally educated people of this country, where those advantages have been in operation for so many centuries, that were practical virtue exactly to keep pace with civilization, we might look for its perfection in the British empire.

It is admitted that polygamy exists among the negroes, but prostitution, in the disgusting shapes it presents itself in this country, is unknown; adultery, if such a term can be applied to a violation of a verbal engagement, or of implied exclusive possession by another, is by no means so much more frequent, as may be supposed, than the actual crime is here, and where there are so many attendant circumstances to make it truly wicked; incest, which unhappily is not quite unknown in Europe, is never heard of among negroes; and it is interesting to know that they do not only object to sexual intercourse between relatives, but commonly disallow of it between those who have been shipmates in the same vessel from Africa; as they form an attachment for each other resembling that of a brother and sister, and which is prohibitory of further intimacy. Of this, many instances have come to the writer's knowledge, and among others, that of a boy and girl, which he bought in 1808; they were remarkably fine well-looking young people, and were brought up as house servants;

at a suitable period, they formed connexions, as their fancies dictated, but always took a most lively interest in each other's welfare, both in sickness and in health. Having to dispose of them preparatory to quitting the island, a few months since, they were consulted as to their wishes upon the subject, when the young woman said she did not care where she lived, provided it was near her shipmate; they were desired to seek situations for themselves, and speedily obtained, he a master, and she a mistress in Spanish Town; and where it afforded to the writer sincere delight to know that they were perfectly happy. It is with no small pleasure he states, that among six or eight servants, three of whom were Africans, brought up in his house, he never experienced either lying or thieving; they had a proud sense of truth and honesty, and scorned falsehood, even in the way of equivocation; and could be trusted to any of the buildings where valuable articles were stored, without hazard. They were all baptized, except one man, who had an invincible objection to it.

The author of the Appeal is shocked that we should have detained the negroes for two centuries in slavery and pagan darkness. Did this country, at the commencement of that period, possess the portion of civil and religious liberty she has since attained, or was she not, for the greater part of one of those centuries, nearly deprived of both? Is there any thing more stupid, more wild, or more ridiculous, in the heathenism of the negroes, than what then appeared in the superstition of the catholics?—or what was evinced in the maniacal enthusiasm of the saints of that period? Is there more of folly or wickedness in the Obeah of the negroes, than in the witchery and wizardism lately practised in Wiltshire to cure fits?—or in the miracles of Prince Hohenlohe, attested by catholic dignitaries, and the charlatanism of quack doctors? The former is scanty among savages, (as they are described,) the latter is but too abundant among the most thinking and best instructed of nations.

Mr. Wilberforce says, " That no attempts " have been made to introduce among them the " Christian institution of marriage." And again, " I have dwelt the longer, and insisted the " more strongly on the universal want of the " marriage institution among the slaves." In the preface to " The Substance of a Debate, &c." the Society assert of marriage, that " It cannot " be said to exist among them!" " They are " still denied the blessings of the marriage " tie!"

In the Appendix D. of the same pamphlet

we have, " The very first step towards improve-
" ment is yet to be made; there is, even at *this*
" *moment*, no marriage tie among 800,000 Bri-
" tish subjects; not only is marriage not re-
" quired or enforced, it is absolutely discou-
" raged." " In every country in the universe,
" however barbarous and uncivilized, the insti-
" tution of marriage exists, and its obligations
" are understood and respected ;" and further on,
" even in pagan Africa, though polygamy exists,
" the marriage contract is held sacred, and is
" guarded by the most formidable sanctions;
" among the slaves in the West Indies alone, of
" the whole human race, the marriage state is
" yet to be instituted."

By what sophistry the gross falsehoods
contained in the above passages is to be ex-
plained or defended, it is difficult to conceive, as
the following extracts are made from the self-
same pamphlet, and prove the former to be
malicious and premeditated. In the Appendix
F. we find, " Returns have been made to the
" House of Commons, by which it would appear,
" that in the last fourteen years, 3,596 legal
" marriages had been celebrated in the island
" of Jamaica ;" and the Rev. Mr. Bridge's Reply
was before the Society, wherein, in contradiction to Mr. Wilberforce on this subject, he says,
" This I positively contradict by stating that I

" have myself married 187 couples of negro
" slaves, in my own parish, within the last two
" years; all of whom were encouraged by their
" owners to marry." Matrimony among negroes
has been in progress during some years, especially in Kingston, Spanish Town, St. Andrew,
and St. Thomas in the East. In the latter
parish, the curate, the Rev. J. Stainsby, has informed the writer that scarcely a Sunday
elapsed, but several couples were married by the
rector, the Rev. Mr. Trew. When such disin-
genuous calumny is thus sent forth into the
world by men, many of whom have no local
knowledge of the West Indies, it is to be hoped
that evidence in contradiction to their asser-
tions, from those who have long had such
advantages, will be allowed its proper weight.
The meliorating Act of the Leeward Islands, of
1798, states, " it was unnecessary and even im-
" proper to enforce the celebration of any reli-
" gious rites among slaves, in order to sanctify
" contracts, the faithful performance of which
" could be looked for only by a regular improve-
" ment in religion, morality, and civilization;"
in which statement there is much sound, practical reasoning. Marriage is not *necessarily* a
religious ceremony in all Christian countries; we
may mention, for an instance, Scotland. Sensible
negroes have been known to object to it, as a
solemn religious contract; saying they under-

stood that many of the white people, both there and in England, were as bad afterwards as before marriage.

Matrimony among the free coloured people is now extremely common; all the better class of them in Clarendon are married. What is meant by the marriage contract being held sacred among the Africans it is difficult to figure; as, in ninety-nine parts out of a hundred of that vast continent, the women are domestic slaves, liable to cruelty and torture, to be put to death at pleasure, or immolated at the graves of their deceased husbands; and polygamy prevails throughout that country.

Mr. Wilberforce asserts, that " the almost " universal destitution of moral and religious " instruction among the slaves, is the most seri- " ous of all the vices of the West Indian sys- " tem." Again, " Of late years, various colonial " laws have been passed, professedly with a " view to the promoting of religion among the " slaves; but they are all, I fear, worse than " nullities;" and, " the gift even of the sabbath " is more than the established economics of a " sugar plantation permit even the most inde- " pendent planter to confer, while the law tacitly " sanctions its being wholly withheld from " them."

In opposition to the above statements, several articles are found in " The Substance of the Debate, &c." where Sir G. Rose mentions that he could give proofs that the improved religion of the slaves had already reflected a light upwards, and acted on classes of society above them, producing new feelings and a new impulse; and that in an island where the greatest progress had been made in evangelizing the negroes, institutions were actually in progress, of which the West Indies would not have been regarded as susceptible a few years back. But he was bound to shew he was holding out no illusive hope; a regular improvement in the feelings of the West India proprietors and of their attornies was in rapid progress, as demonstrated by various facts. Sir G. Rose calculates the progress of conversion in this way, viz. 80,000 adults, under the care of, and profiting by the instruction of, the Wesleyans; and 20,000 more in communion with the Moravians, Baptists, and Church of England, forming a total of 100,000, or one-eighth of the whole slave population. The Rev. Mr. Bridges reports, that during his residence of six years in Manchester Parish, he has actually baptized 9,413 negro slaves, many of whom attend church, have learnt the Lord's Prayer and the Ten Commandments, and some so far advanced as to be now disseminating their little stock of religious knowledge on the estates to which they are attached. There were 5,773 slaves baptized in the parish of Hanover, from 1814, to June, 1817.

In the parish of Clarendon, in place of the negroes not being even permitted to devote the Sunday to religious purposes, they are never prevented attending divine service at the churches; and many of them, from properties within a moderate distance of the places of worship, do attend, some pretty regularly, and others occasionally. The Author attended service at the chapel on the parade, in Kingston, so long ago as in March, 1821, and found it crowded with blacks and people of colour, numbers of whom were slaves; most of them had Prayer-Books, and joined in the responses and in the Psalms. Of late years, several additional places of worship have been erected in Kingston, at considerable expence, and are generally well filled with congregations, a great portion of which are slaves.

Is all this nothing? and, being true, does it support Mr. W. in saying, " he does not know " of any *material* improvement that has been " adopted, and that the abuses pointed out by " the abolitionists are still existing *in all their* " *original force?*" That the entire conversion of the negroes to Christianity is not a work of so easy accomplishment as may be imagined, the following fact will prove. In 1802, the chaplain at Cape Coast Castle was a negro, the Rev. Mr. Quaco; he had been brought up in England, and had an university education. On his return to Africa after ordination, it was generally understood among the whites resident at Cape Coast, and by them confidently and publicly asserted, that he became a believer in the fetishes and other barbarous superstitions of the natives.

Education has at least made a beginning among the negroes. How many attend the schools only recently opened in Kingston, upon the Lancasterian system, is not known to the writer; but, as the means of instruction can be had at so low a rate, it may be anticipated that, in the course of the year, considerable numbers will be profiting by them. On most large estates there are some negroes who can read and instruct others; and on going into their houses, as was very frequently the writer's lot to do, elementary books, prints, and rude drawings, were found there.

In the pamphlet entitled " Negro Slavery," under the head of the " Evidence of the Rev. Thomas Cooper," it is stated, " The law of the " island requires that one day in a fortnight, " except during the time of crop, should be " allowed to the slaves, exclusive of Sunday, " for cultivating their provision-grounds. This

" would amount to from fourteen to sixteen days
" in the year. The proprietor of Georgia was,
" however, more liberal than *the law*." It is
desirable to believe that the Reverend Gentle-
man has here rather daringly asserted what the
law is, without having any correct knowledge
upon the subject; than that he should have
done so, after reading the law, which gives the
negroes twenty-six days in the year for working
in their grounds, and that exclusive of Sundays
and holidays, as will be shewn by the following
extract from the Slave Law of Jamaica, of the
year 1816: " That from and after the com-
" mencement of this Act, the slaves belonging
" to, or employed on, every plantation or settle-
" ment shall, over and above the holidays, here-
" inafter to be mentioned, be allowed one day
" in every fortnight to cultivate their own pro-
" vision-grounds, exclusive of Sunday, except
" during the time of crop, under the penalty of
" twenty pounds, to be recovered against the
" overseer or person having the care of such
" slaves: *Provided always*, that the number of
" days, so allowed to the slaves for the cultiva-
" tion of their grounds, *shall be at least twenty-*
" *six in the year*."

Mr. Cooper says, " the slaves are addicted
" to thieving;" but he adds, " that to this vice,
" in some cases, they are strongly tempted, by

D

" the unreasonable conduct of the planters them-
" selves. These generally refuse to sell any of
" their sugar in the island ; the consequence is,
" that those who are not sugar planters can
" procure it only in a concealed and smuggled
" way, in the negro market, where it is all stolen
" sugar." Mr. Cooper, who refused to buy any
such, was obliged to tell the attorney of Georgia,
" if he would not allow him to have some
" sugar on the estate, he must send to London
" for it." Such is the evidence of one who
should not be deficient in that moral and religious culture he had immediately before been
deploring the want of in the negro ; and yet it
will be difficult to consider it a practical exem-
plification of such attainments, if the following
statement be correct.

On many estates, the proprietor or attorney is pledged to ship all the sugar beyond
what is required for the consumption of the
negroes and white people upon the estate
(and which is no inconsiderable quantity) to
Europe; consequently, a retailing of sugar
upon the plantation is inadmissible. Out of
twenty estates situated in the parish of Clarendon, there were no less than ten where sugar
was disposed of in quantities of fifty pounds
weight and upwards, to coffee planters and
others. The Author's family was supplied, at

various times, from seven different properties.
And further, if Mr. Cooper was so unfortunately
placed, as not to be able to get sugar from Georgia, or any neighbouring plantation, he need not
have gone quite so far as the London market for
it, while the towns of Lucea and Montego Bay
were somewhat easier of access. It is not easy
to understand what Mr. Cooper means by
" those who are not sugar planters obtaining it
" in a concealed and smuggled way;" the writer
never knew or heard of such a thing; and as to
the sale of stolen sugar in markets, he has seen
many negro markets, very many times, but
never saw sugar offered for sale in any of them.

To say " the negro is robbed of his liberty,
" and cannot marry," are hardly Gospel truths;
as he never possessed the former, in our accep-
tation of the term, and the latter he is not
restricted from, as has been already shewn.
The insinuation that " a *third* person can step in
" and disannul the holy league," has but little of
Christian charity, and must, it is believed, be
unfounded in experience there, however frequently something very like it takes place *here*.
Mr. Cooper says, " White women, who are
" owners of slaves, will in general, without any
" scruple, order their slaves to be flogged; *and*
" *some of them will even stand by to see them*
" *stripped bare, and punished in the usual disgust-*
" *ing manner.*" The latter part of this paragraph

is a most heavy charge against the delicacy and humanity of the ladies of Jamaica; and Mr. Cooper would have rewarded them properly by exposing their names. The Author was seventeen years longer there than Mr. Cooper, and was acquainted with a very considerable number of females so circumstanced, but certainly never knew an instance in support of Mr. Cooper's assertion.

And this is called the "unbiassed testimony "of a respectable Christian minister!" Does it not rather resemble that of a disappointed, discontented man? inasmuch as it is characterized by exaggeration and incorrectness. It is not intended to question Mr. Cooper's mode of discharging his duties upon Georgia, but it has not unfrequently happened that gentlemen so situated upon estates, have been apt to interfere with the necessary subordination, upon the properties where they resided, by operating upon the minds of the slaves in such a manner as to establish an *imperium in imperio* of the most dangerous description.

The Author considers it unnecessary to reply to the passages which have been culled out of Dr. Williamson's book, because they regard things as they were, and not as they are; it being many years since Dr. Williamson left Spanish Town, previous to which he had not been for a long time resident in St. Thomas in the Vale, the scene of many of his remarks.

Mr. Wilberforce's assertion, repeated over and over again as it has been, that the Registry Acts are ineffectual to prevent the violation of the Abolition Laws, is strange indeed, if he means to include Jamaica in the general charge; as the Author has been resident there, from the period of the abolition until very recently, and does not believe a single instance of their infraction to have taken place. The only attempt which was ever made of that nature was detected and prosecuted, and the criminals punished, under a law passed by the Jamaica Legislature since the abolition.

Mr. Wilberforce views very lightly the West Indian's apprehension of ruin, " as being " alive to imaginary dangers, and assiduous in " endeavouring to inspire alarm in the mother " country." In Appendix B, the Society say, " Is there then, we shall be asked, no danger of " commotion among the slaves in our colonies? " Undoubtedly there is ; but not from the efforts " which may be made in Parliament for their " relief; of these it would scarcely, we appre- " hend, be too much to say, that they know " almost as little as the cattle and sheep in " Smithfield knew of Mr. Martin's benevolent

" and persevering efforts to protect them from
" the cruelty of man." And in Appendix X,
" The alarms which are sedulously creating at
" the present moment, to serve an obvious pur-
" pose, by rumours of apprehended insurrection,
" and which new plots may even *be got up to*
" *magnify*. Plots issuing, like the former plots,
" in the destruction, not of any white life, but
" of abundance of black lives. These rumours
" of plots, and these paragraphs of alarm, are
" quite familiar to all who lived during the slave
" trade controversy; there was a regular impor-
" tation of them every year, and so there will
" be again."

The writers of the preceding passages must
well know that the negro population of the
West Indies is now composed of very different
elements to what it was at former periods of
alarm. At present they are mostly creoles,
shrewd, intelligent people; the servants are not,
as heretofore, Africans, unacquainted with our
language, but understand every word that is
said in conversation at table, and at other times;
in fact, they have now minds, and have been for
some time acquiring moral, in addition to their
physical strength.

It is just as well known to the authors of
the Report and Appendixes, that the negroes in

the colonies have not been left (like the cattle
in Smithfield market) in ignorance of the efforts
of their *soi disant* advocates. It will be shewn,
when the late events in Demerara are investi-
gated, that they have been stimulated by active
instruments to revolt. Will these gentlemen
say where and when, within the last twenty
years, in the West India colonies, there have
been any indications, of revolt we will not say,
but of an unquiet or discontented spirit, ex-
cepting upon occasions when interference with
them and their regulations, by other means than
those of the Colonial Legislatures, has been immediately impending? The insinuation of *get-
ting up plots*, and the almost declared regret that
the lives of the whites have not on such occasions been sacrificed, are sufficient indications of
the spirit which animates these benevolent gentlemen.

In Appendix D. the condition of the
Haytians is thus drawn, but no authorities
are cited: " We find they are improving in
" the arts of civilized life, protected by equal
" laws, engaged in the pursuits of peaceful
" industry, adhering to the profession, at least,
" of Christianity, and competently discharging
" every duty attaching to them as citizens
" and members of a well-regulated commu-
" nity." That this sketch of the Haytians

has some colouring from the fancy, seems very probable; or the improvement which has taken place among them must have been rapid indeed, as it is not long since the *well-regulated community* was a severe military despotism, in which the sword was substituted for the whip as the stimulus to labour; the fruits of which were, it was pretended, divided into three equal portions; one third to the government, one to the manager, and the other to the labourers. But how was this latter paid? After arbitrarily fixing the amount, did they receive it in produce, or its fair value in money? No: but in supplying their wants of clothing, spirits, &c. of such quality, and at such prices, as the manager might determine.

From all that has come to the Author's knowledge since his return to England, it would seem that merchants and proprietors of estates, resident in this country, are extremely deficient in knowledge of the actual condition of the slaves; and there are numerous particulars of local detail, of which any thing like correct information can only be obtained by actual residence. It is highly to be regretted that owners of estates do not go out to their plantations, in place of relieving their consciences by yielding to the arguments of their enemies, and by so doing committing acts of self-destruction. In taking such a step, they would afford the best proof of the sincere interest they take in the happiness of their slaves, by devoting their personal aid and attention to the work of amelioration. At present, many among them prefer living here in apathy, to making exertions which involve hazard and difficulty; and while they write letters which embarrass and paralyze the exertions of their representatives, almost invariably want money,—more money to support their idle expenditure; and this is to be made consistent with scanty returns from diminished crops and low prices. Although there are numerous holders of West India property who do not come within the censure included in the above observations, it is a most serious evil that there should be so many who do.

It is hoped that the candid reader and lover of truth will admit, that what has appeared in these pages proves satisfactorily, not only that something has been done in mitigation of slavery, but that in the last fifteen years much has been accomplished; and more would, most likely, have been effected, but for the very distressed state of the planters, many of whom are deeply in debt, cultivate their estates at vast expence, and, from the low price of sugar, and obtaining scarcely any thing for rum, derive from them, in many instances, little or no income. The bringing forward the project of emancipation at such a moment, is doubly cruel; and however the friends of that measure may vaunt their love of justice and humanity, there is too much reason to believe that, should the consequence be a general massacre of the whites, and the ruin of the colonies, the maxim of Rochefoucault, " il " y a quelque chose dans les malheurs de nos " meilleurs amis qui ne nous déplaît pas," would not be without its appropriate application, in the feelings of these philanthropists, who would probably bear the misfortunes of the sufferers with great Christian fortitude.

This stoical indifference, however, could not long continue to be the feeling of the British public; for the influence of the colonies upon the manufactures, wealth, revenue, and naval strength of the empire, would, within a very short time, be sensibly estimated and regretted. Nor ought the public to consider the case of the colonists as insulated, since, if Great Britain acts with consistent justice, she must indemnify her suffering subjects for the sacrifices which she is demanding from them.

It is said the work of amelioration does not go on fast enough; such is the opinion loudly and passionately expressed on this side of the water, where (as is the case with learned pro-

fessors, lecturing dogmatically on the conta-
giousness of yellow fever, which they have
never seen,) they are so much better informed
than those who may have spent half a century
in the West Indies. Whether more ought to
have been done in the same period, is matter of
opinion; that there is a disposition to meet and
forward the views of Government, as lately
expressed, so far as they are consistent and
practicable, there is little room to doubt; and
had not the object of emancipation been prema-
turely introduced, the desired good would have
been of more easy attainment, and the present
perilous state of things would have been hap-
pily avoided.

Hampton, November 1, 1823.

TABLE I.—*Referred to in p. 15.*

Name.	Date of Admission.	Disease.	Prescriptions, day of 182	Discharged.	Result.

TABLE II.—*Referred to in p. 16.*

No.	Name.	Age.	When reported Pregnant.	Period of Pregnancy	If first or what succeeding Pregnancy	Number of Miscarriages.	Number of Children living.	Date of Delivery or Miscarriages.	Sex of Child.	State of Child at end of Month.	State of Mother at end of Month.	Miscellaneous Remarks.

The above is the form of the Table described by the Author in his evidence before the Committee of the House of Assembly, and was attached to his Practical Remarks, published in Jamaica. Similar Tables were appended to some Hospital Journals he had printed by Messrs. Longman & Co.

RETURN